Praise for *How the Wind Moves*

"*How The Wind Moves* is an amazing anthology that will take you on a romantic journey with the beautiful way these poets intertwine their deeply felt stories in an unexpected format called 'split sequence.' This excellent way of layering poetic conversations will enthrall you. It is a must-have for your library."

—**Garry Gay**, founder of Haiku Poets of Northern California (HPNC) and creator of rengay

"*How The Wind Moves* is a stunning collection of poems that uses glowing imagery and beautiful metaphors to give readers a sprinkle of hope. It reveals the upside of both little and big moments in life. Those who wish to learn more about split sequences will find it a priceless resource."

—**John J. Han, Ph.D.,** editor of *Cantos* and *Fireflies' Light*

"Christine L. Villa has brought together a number of contemporary poets well known for their short-form poetry. In this volume, you can see how poets can work together to create a piece of work greater than its two individual halves. This is an important book, the first anthology of its kind. It will be exciting to see how this short form of poetry evolves from here."

—**Patricia McGuire**, managing editor of *Poetry Pea*

How the Wind Moves

Velvet Dusk Publishing

Copyright © 2023 Velvet Dusk Publishing
Artwork copyright © 2023 Christine L. Villa

First published in 2023 by Velvet Dusk Publishing
Sacramento, CA

All rights reserved. This book or any portion thereof may not be reproduced or used in any manner whatsoever without the express written permission of the publisher, except for the use of brief quotations in a book review.

ISBN: 978-1-958753-09-5

For all the adventurous poets

Acknowledgments

A bow of infinite respect and boundless gratitude to Peter Jastermsky for creating the split sequence and for giving me support and guidance from my first collaboration with him up to the completion of this book.

Huge thanks also to Bryan Rickert for reaching out to Peter Jastermsty and eventually writing with him a collection of collaborative split sequences, *Just Dust and Stone*. This book ignited my passionate pursuit to collaborate with others.

A bouquet of appreciation to all the 46 poets whose unique voices made each page of this anthology shimmer like iridescent leaves in the wind.

Special thanks to all the editors who published our collaborations and the following editors who, for the first time, opened their doors for collaborative split sequences.

Saima Afreen of *Narrow Road*
Hemapriya Chellappan of *Failed Haiku*
Susan Beth Furst of *Behold*
John J. Han of *Cantos* and *Fireflies' Light*
Tia Haynes of *Prune Juice*
Katie Lynn Johnston of *Mulberry Literary*
Jim Lewis of *Verse-Virtual*
Clare MacQueen of *MacQueen's Quinterly*
Patricia McGuire of *Poetry Pea Journal*

Tom Sacramona of *Frogpond*
Caroline Skanne of *hedgerow: a journal of small poems*
Kathleen Trocmet of *Scarlet Dragonfly Journal*
Steve Wilkinson of *The Bamboo Hut*

Last but not least, profuse thanks to Susan Weaver for her help in editing and proofreading.

Contents

Foreword 11

Introduction 13

Flutter of the Heart 17

Cracks 31

Setting Free 43

Improvising 57

Linked 67

Broken Peace 79

After 89

New Beginnings 99

Afterword 113

Participating Poets 115

Publishing Credits 125

About the Editor/Poet 127

Foreword

In early 2018 I was sitting in a dentist's chair with the first copy of the short-lived journal *ephemerae* in my hands. Trying to keep my mind off the immediate circumstances, I started flipping through the pages. As it happened, I found more than what I bargained for on page 35. The first split sequence poem I had ever seen. A three-line haiku and, under each line, an individual haiku. All were written by Peter Jastermsky. Hours later, pain meds wearing off, I found myself on Facebook messenger talking all about this new thing with Peter, a complete stranger.

But why something new? What do split sequences offer that other, more traditional forms don't have? Many other forms of linked verse have a lot of traditions and rules. While split sequences are not free-for-alls, they do not have to be as structured or formal as renku. Using link and shift in a very similar way, split sequences have the ability to break free from the mold and express other ideas related to the development of small narratives. Since the opening haiku is present at every level of the poem, the secondary haiku should not just link to the individual line above it but also to the original haiku and all the other secondary haiku as a whole. Creating more than just a dialogue between two poets, this multiple-linking idea should challenge writers and readers to think about haiku collaboration in new and interesting ways.

How the Wind Moves is a collection of linked poems that explores and pushes the boundaries of what is possible with the split sequence form. Showcasing a wide range of poets representing different facets of our haiku community, Christine L. Villa has co-authored a rich body of work. This collection features sequences on a broad variety of topics, and every page provides new ideas and voices. A collection that truly offers something for everyone and gives us plenty of opportunity to explore something new.

Having curated the first book of collaborative split sequences and being an accomplished poet and editor, Villa is perfectly situated to be the poet/editor to bring us this far-reaching new anthology. It serves as a tutorial with great depth and scope and helps move the form forward into the haiku community. Having such a wide array of co-authors, she proves this new form can find its home at every level of our global haiku community.

Motivated by her love of poetry, Villa gives us what is, I hope, the first of many opportunities to explore, not just the possibilities of traditional haiku, but the potential of what haiku can become—fresh avenues of thought and the playfulness that comes with doing something new. That is truly what *How the Wind Moves* embodies as a collection. An adventurous step forward that you will have no regrets about reading.

—Bryan Rickert

Introduction

"I love collaboration of all kinds, and I love the way that collaboration pulls me in directions I wouldn't go if I was working on my own."
—James Franco

I knew I was smitten with a new form of poetry the moment I laid my eyes on *Just Dust and Stone*, a collection of collaborative split sequences by Peter Jastermsky and Bryan Rickert. I didn't want to pass up the opportunity of publishing it through Velvet Dusk Publishing, and though I was experiencing a dry spell in my haiku writing, I was also tempted to try my hand at split sequences.

Thanks to Peter! After I plucked up the courage to ask him, he instantly agreed to write with me my first collaborative split sequence, and from then on, I have been utterly hooked. I love how a seed haiku twists and turns and blossoms into wonderful linked verses. The process is a journey full of adventures and surprises.

For this anthology, I was fortunate to be able to write with 46 poets. Just when I thought I had run out of things to write about, a new idea or inspiration would spring forth from alternate responses. Like a leaf, I bent, swayed, fluttered, and flew, depending on where the wind would take me. How the wind moved was unpredictable, somehow determined by our own unique and universal experiences and the extent of our imagination. Each split sequence was a trip through memory or to places I had never been before. If I had written the split sequences alone, would I have dared to go beyond the familiar?

As my collection of collaborative split sequences grew, I envisioned more poets writing with other poets and more journals accepting this new form of poetry. I was ecstatic that several editors started opening their doors to split sequences as well as collaborative split sequences when I submitted to them for the first time.

It's not a surprise for me that it didn't take long before more people caught the "fever." As I write this, I am already making a list of poets for the next anthology. But before that comes into play, I hope this first anthology serves its purpose, to nudge you to learn something new, explore collaborating with fellow poets, or simply enjoy the varied voices on these pages, including the mixed media art I created to enhance your reading experience.

—Christine L. Villa

How the Wind Moves

Flutter of the Heart

In a Season

our first hello

*sun beam
bird tweets inside
a carved pumpkin*

the scent of autumn

*picked apples
on her jeans
bits of hay*

in his scarf

*taste of cinnamon
a reminder to return
his call*

Tia Haynes
Christine L. Villa

New Journeys

dappled shade

> *winding road*
> *not knowing how far*
> *to trust you*

our first walk

> *freesia scent*
> *your footprints move*
> *closer to mine*

together

> *baby steps*
> *little by little*
> *a fresh start*

Christine L. Villa
Bryan Rickert

Imprints

throwing stones

park bench
our thoughts
spoken out loud

how your ripples

bus ticket
the date stamped
in our history

meet mine

good night kiss
the jiggle of keys
in my hand

Tia Haynes
Christine L. Villa

The First Note

music festival

   tuning up
   a soft ring
   of overtones

the scent

   barbecue smoke
   the stolen glances
   on our first date

of bluegrass

   orange blossoms
   fiddling around
   until the kiss

Christine L. Villa
Peter Jastermsky

All It Takes

field of sunflowers—

airport arrivals
our eyes lock
in a sea of faces

who could forget

a flood of memories
no recall why
we stopped speaking

your smile

revolving door
how we go back
to where we left off

Mary Kendall
Christine L. Villa

Spring Rendezvous

flower moon

   his first touch
   after so many years
   spring drizzle

releasing the butterfly

   soft kisses
   two bodies breathing
   in tandem

in her obi

   sea waves
   from her back curve
   symphony of love

Christine L. Villa
Hifsa Ashraf

Stay

once more a taste

> *wild cherry*
> *you said your lips*
> *can't wait*

of how it used to be

> *burning love*
> *scar by scar*
> *the stars collide*

night jasmine

> *spilled wine*
> *we linger longer*
> *with no regrets*

Elisa Theriana
Christine L. Villa

October Winds

mountain lake

*pine trees
it starts with
a whisper*

I wash my hands

the long reach
of her promise
evening sun

in starlight

*gentle breeze
a hilltop house
much clearer*

Dave Read
Christine L. Villa

Flutter of the Heart

prairie sky

   morning stroll
   his last name rolls off
   my tongue

the rippling voices

   my reflection
   on the lotus pond
   a drift of sunlight

of summer grass

   butterfly wings
   I practice saying
   the words "I do"

Chen-ou Liu
Christine L. Villa

Cracks

Prelude

late summer sky

*the way you kiss
the mole on my shoulder
lilac afterglow*

a part of me

serenades
through the balcony
blossom wind

still blue

*day moon
how long will it be
this time*

Hifsa Ashraf
Christine L. Villa

Embellishment

cannelloni

   wedding toast
   splashes of tomato sauce
   on his tie

the stuff he adds

   the motive
   behind many compliments
   whipped frosting

to his stories

   pillow talk
   whispered hopes for
   our happy ending

Christine L. Villa
Carol Judkins

The Morning After

two stars

> *evening walk*
> *lost in the stare*
> *of your eyes*

in a puddle

> *invisible rain*
> *a bus stop's*
> *wet kiss*

for a moment

> *scrambled eggs*
> *you say it's you*
> *not me*

Al Peat
Christine L. Villa

The Bait

crackle on the radio

   a country song
   found in the bottom
   of his beer

changing the topic

   steak or pork chop
   I start to sizzle
   in his eyes

so he would listen

   long way home
   a grease spot spreading
   on the take-out bag

Christine L. Villa
Terri L. French

Stuck

traffic jam

   looming shadows
   a giraffe family
   strolls by

we lose the thread

   fallen asleep
   my mind swings
   tree to tree

of our conversation

   migrating geese
   the dialogue between
   wings and wind

Christine L. Villa
Sherry Grant

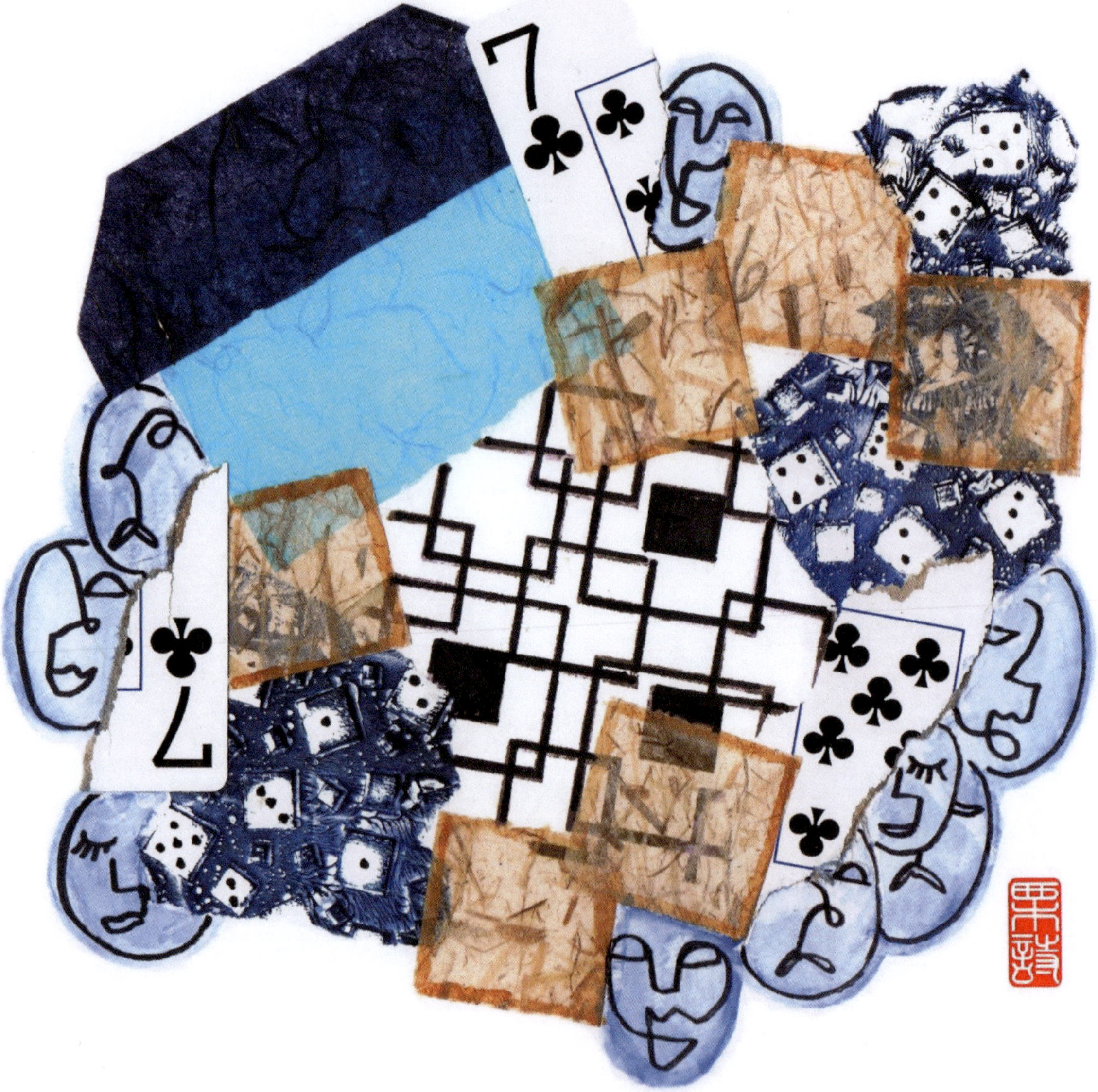

Dream Home

new house

deck of cards
we gamble on
our dreams

vultures perch

family and friends
the seesaw of support
and warnings

on the garbage bin

cardboard boxes
the weight of starting
fresh

Claire Vogel Camargo
Christine L. Villa

Unfrayed Seams

spinning room

   garbage disposal
   I muffle the sound
   of his voice

I hold on to the edge

   play date
   taking my time out
   in the shower

of my sanity

   bedtime story
   I make up my own
   happy ending

Bona M. Santos
Christine L. Villa

Cracks

home late

> *waning moon*
> *a sliver of light beneath*
> *the bedroom door*

her clattering bracelets

> *garbage pickup*
> *no sleep has taken me*
> *by dawn*

when she lies

> *I dare not ask*
> *another question*
> *bitter coffee*

Pris Campbell
Christine L. Villa

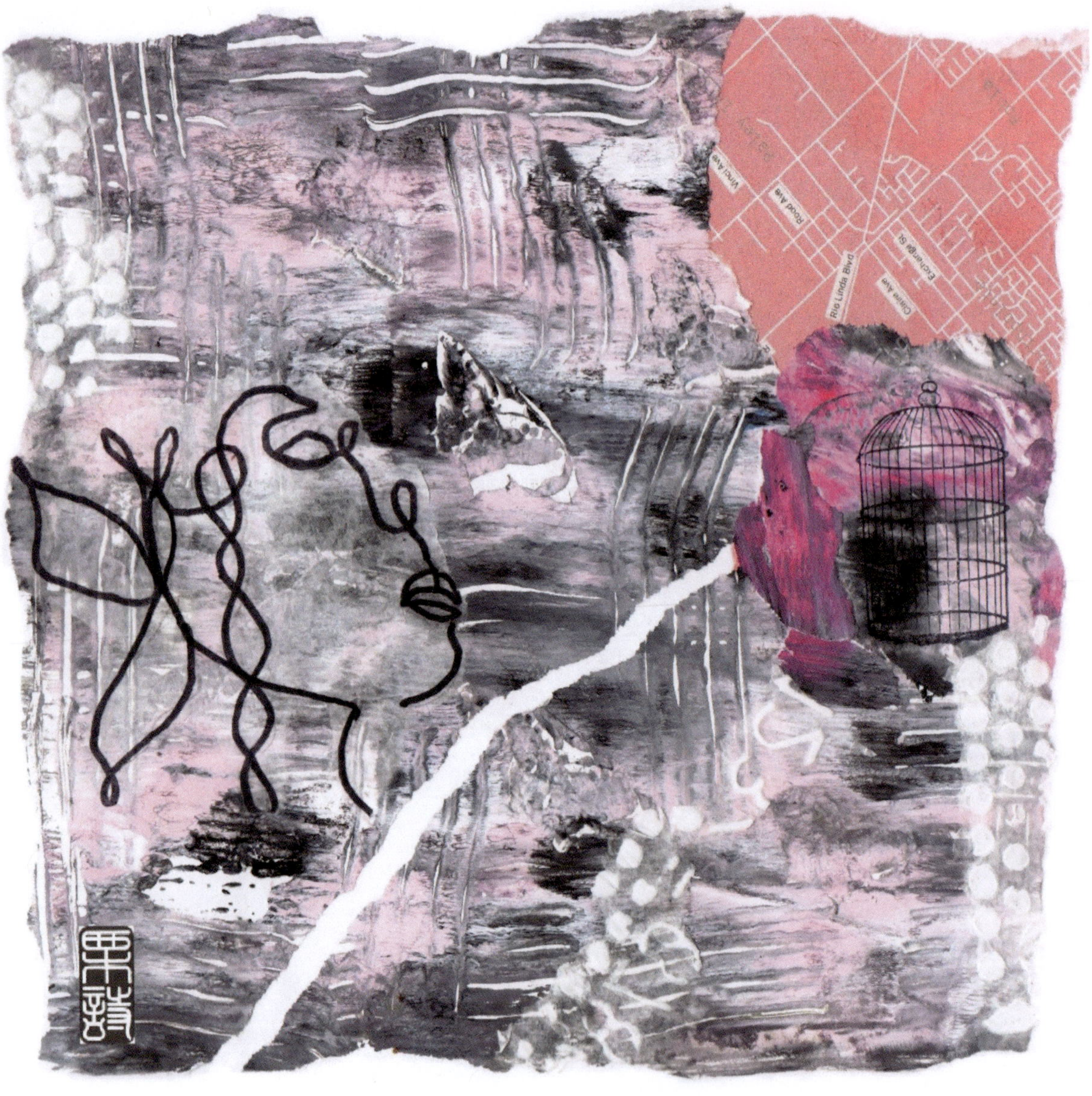
Vinci Ave
Rood Ave
Rio Linda Blvd
Exchange St
Clyde Ave

Setting Free

On the Brink

cloud formation

*a snail glides
on the horizon
false spring*

where do I begin

hoping for
a second opinion
cliff's edge

telling you

*how to love
yourself first
pink camellia*

Christine L. Villa
Hemapriya Chellappan

Signpost

broken zipper

> *rain clouds . . .*
> *stuck again at a*
> *fork in the road*

it doesn't matter

> worn out sneakers
> this urge to give up
> the fight

how hard I try

> *so far,*
> *so good . . .*
> *migrating cranes*

Christine L. Villa
Carol Judkins

46

Gridlock

battle lines

    broken fence
    you should know by now
    when I need space

so I'm like my mother

    mean girls
    spitting out
    the cherry pips

get over it

    bad tattoo
    not everything
    can be fixed

Hazel Hall
Christine L. Villa

How the Wind Moves

escalation

   whistling kettle
   no way left to hide
   the truth

on the fire escape

   knock on the door
   our neighbor says she hears
   every word

loud coos of pigeons

   unclipped wings
   the freedom to be
   myself

Robin Anna Smith
Christine L. Villa

Elimination

finding out

   a foreign scent
   his side of the bed
   distant fog

what doesn't work

   perched heron
   on the watch for
   a phone beep

ring rash

   tinder profile
   waxing over
   her tan line

Christine L. Villa
Michael H. Lester

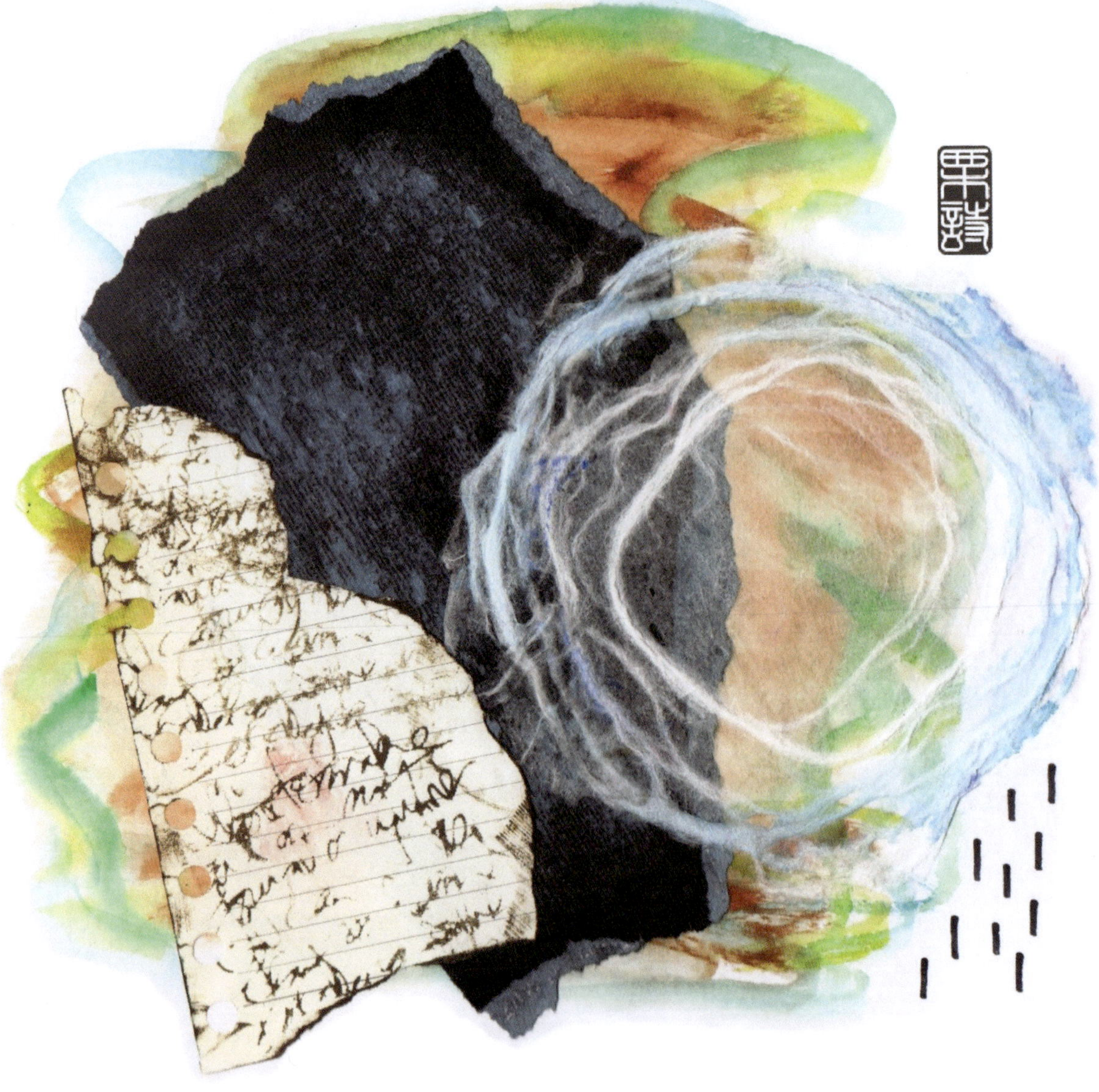

Damage Control

cracks on the moon

   arguments
   the ripped pages
   of a diary

I tiptoe around

   fall litter
   I cleanse
   my aura

his ego

   prickly cactus
   finding no cushion
   for this breakup

Vandana Parashar
Christine L. Villa

Second Split

drizzle-blasted

   another argument
   a sliver of us
   chips away

we are no longer

   just an echo
   along the canyon
   were we just that

(as) fairytales

   our story ends
   on a cliffhanger
   a roll of thunder

Alan Summers
Christine L. Villa

Setting Free

peruvian lily

   no longer tracing
   my name on his chest
   unscented night

all those scars

   getting deeper
   into the moonlight
   my heartache

I take for granted

   lavender tea
   after the last sip
   I whisper goodbye

Hifsa Ashraf
Christine L. Villa

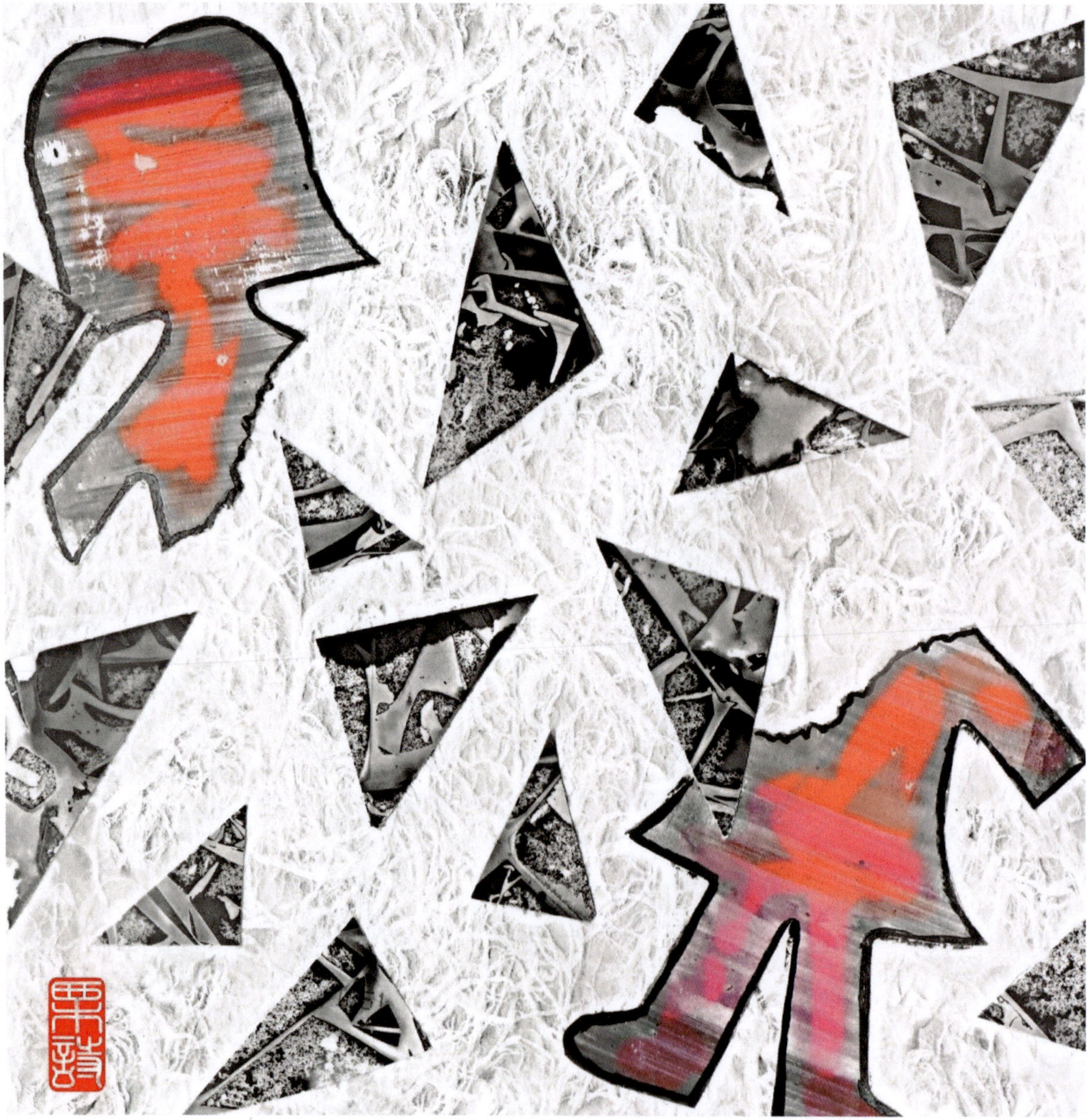

Unfriended

paper doll

> *the first time*
> *you call me sissy*
> *gossamer moon*

I cut you

> *splintered glass*
> *the dagger look*
> *I give you*

out of my life

> *blackballed*
> *I won't give you*
> *another thought*

Christine L. Villa
Susan Burch

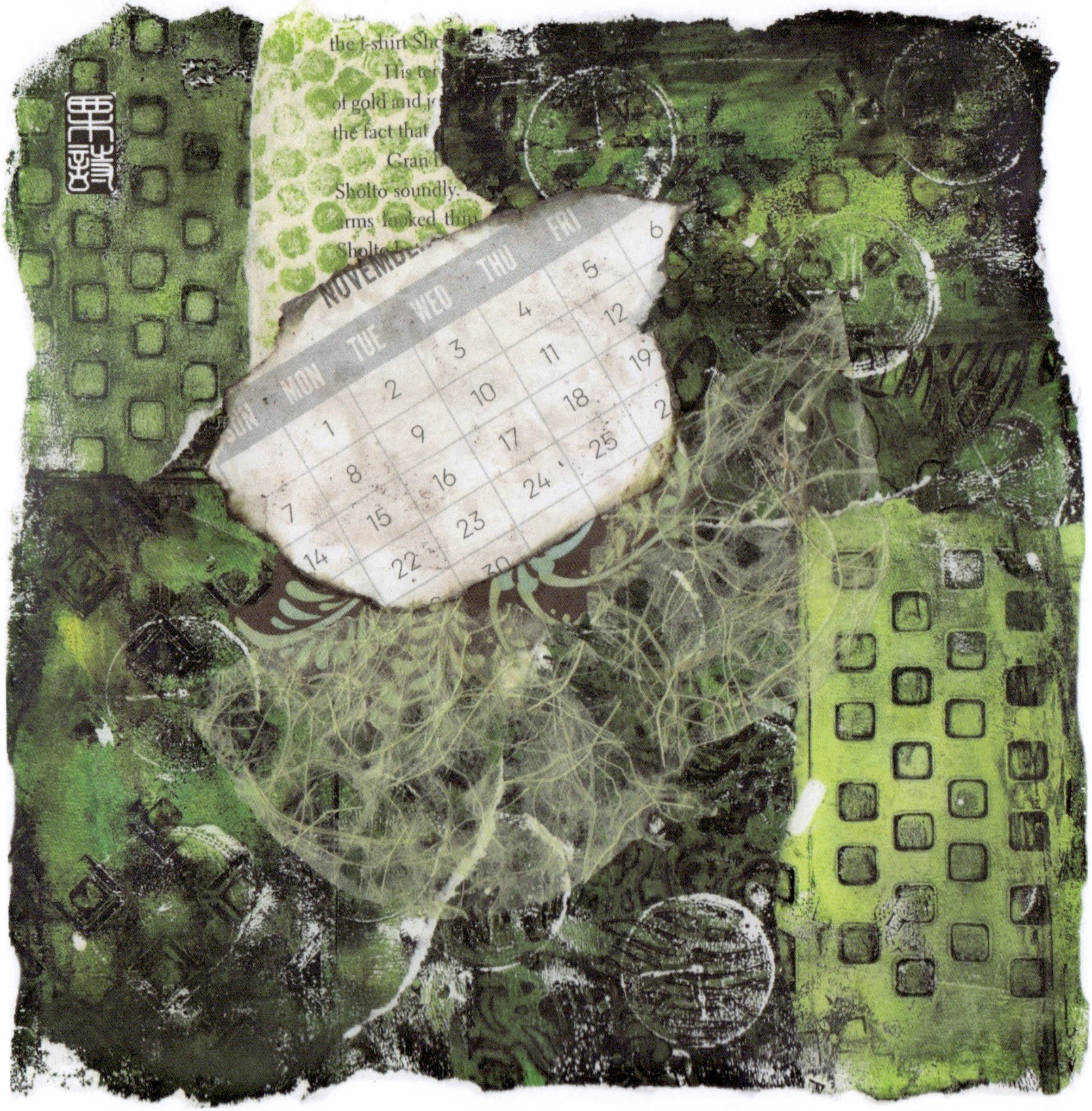

Improvising

Circling the Drain

revolving door

> *wrinkled sheets*
> *back to the hotel room*
> *alone*

memories return

> *dropping the soap*
> *what the shower*
> *won't wash away*

in a roundabout way

> *unreturned call*
> *the expiration*
> *of an apology*

Peter Jastermsky
Christine L. Villa

Waiting

filigree leaves

> *stashed away*
> *the silver earrings*
> *she used to wear*

the old calendar

> empty months
> a single chair
> at the dusty table

still on the fridge

> *waiting*
> *to be signed*
> *divorce papers*

Christine L. Villa
Cynthia Anderson

is here.
match his eyes and
all Seelie Court
Court. In the
up and around. Did he
What is it?"
magic, but
Sholto
genetics

After Lucinda?

six lakes

*the same image
staring back at me
water reflection*

I don my merman scales

*a taste of something
from a long-ago incident
a flutter of memory*

bubble by bubble

*scar after scar
I slowly learn to swim
against the tide*

Alan Summers
Christine L. Villa

Insomnia

winter night . . .

> *cold moon rising . . .*
> *I attempt to forget*
> *ghosts of the past*

walking faster than me

> New Year's resolutions
> the lies I tell
> myself

my own shadow

> *dark alcove —*
> *my inner child crouches*
> *where no one sees*

Christine L. Villa
Hazel Hall

Improvising

morning dew

*early riser
scattered clouds
scatter the light*

how my worries dissolve

alone time
dipping my brush
in water

into this moment

*wind bends the pine
these longer days
without you*

Christine L. Villa
Cynthia Anderson

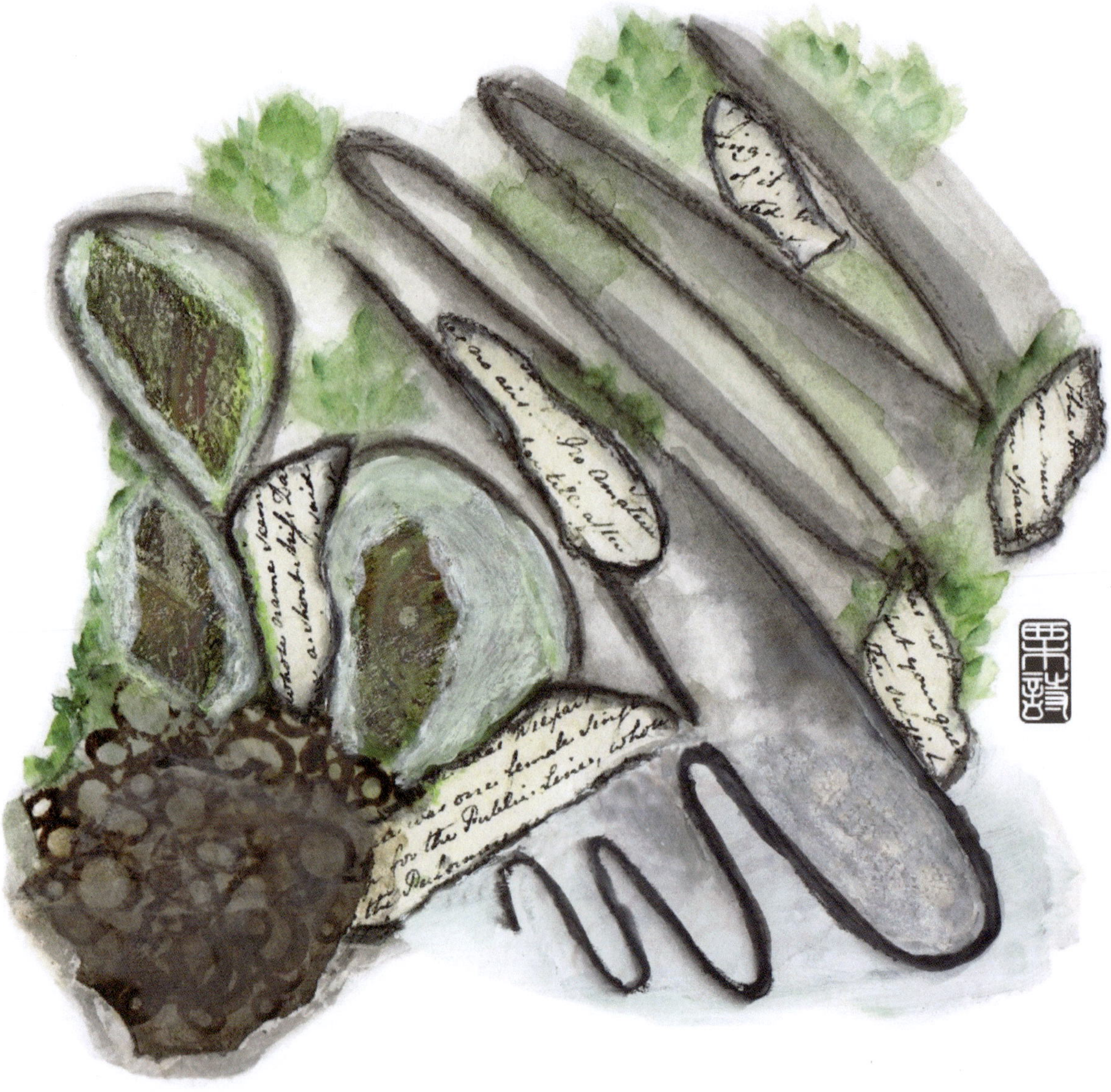

Over and Over

lichens

   rocky coasts
   the things I do
   to survive

pretending to know

   from a cup of tea
   all the answers to life's
   great conundrums

something i don't

   early morning fog
   the permanent streaks
   on my windshield

Michael Henry Lee
Christine L. Villa

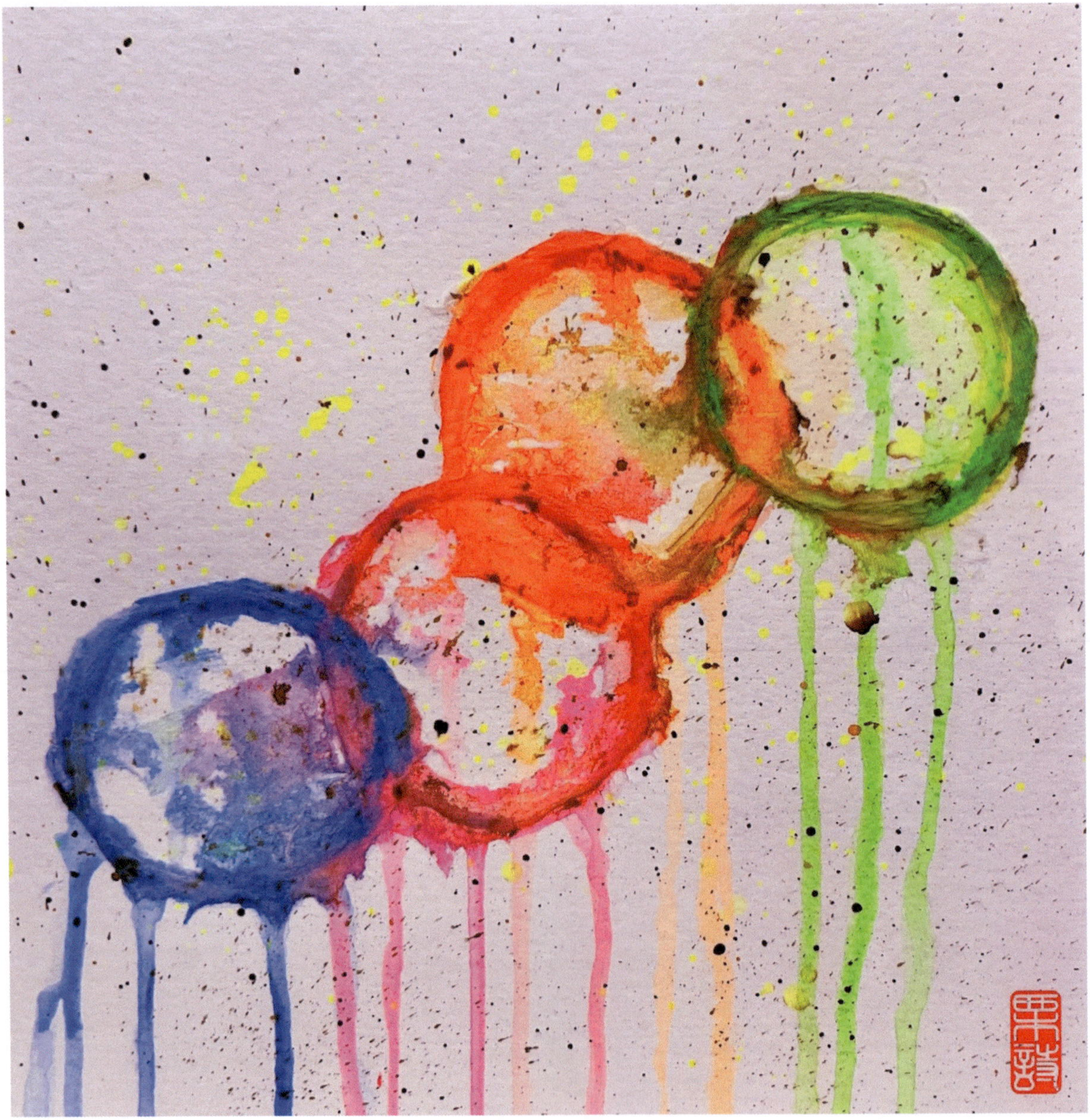

Linked

Self-Soothing

stick for arms

   long talks
   with an imaginary friend
   missing dad

a snowman doesn't return

   snowmelt
   his come-and-go
   through my life

a toddler's hug

   lullaby
   the white noise
   of a heater fan

Bryan Rickert
Christine L. Villa

Thursday's Child

another bed

>*a blinking neon sign*
>*outside the window*
>*Paradise motel*

another foster home

>waking up
>to a new set of rules
>beer for breakfast

snow on snow

>*the velvet curtain*
>*slowly rises*
>*Tchaikovsky's Nutcracker*

Christine L. Villa
Linda Papanicolaou

Linked

before they fly

> *streetlamps*
> *the cry of birdlings*
> *at midnight*

in opposite directions

> driving north
> as the geese go south
> divorce papers

children

> *a bracelet*
> *with all their names*
> *holding it together*

Deborah P Kolodji
Christine L. Villa

Letting Go

daffodil breeze

    somersaults
    sticky weeds stick
    to his cowlick

remembering again

    church bell
    a dragonfly and I
    pause

how you left me

    wings
    of a fledgling
    first day of school

Christine L. Villa
Christina Chin

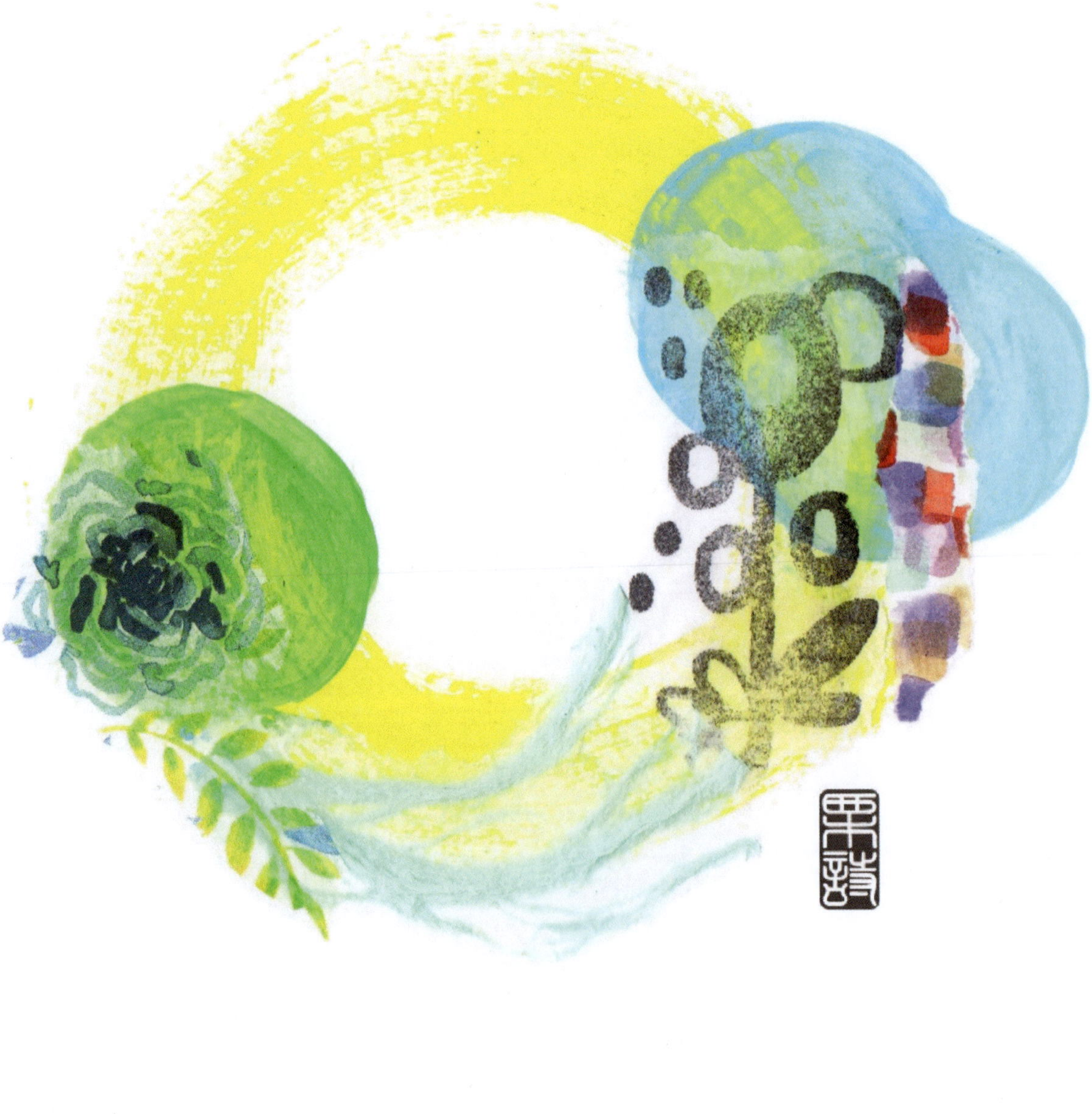

Lineage

family ties

    it always
    winds down to you
    summer river

the horizontal roots

    time capsule
    we pry the lid off
    our youth

of rubber trees

    tire swing
    our laughter brighter
    than the sun

Debbie Strange
Christine L. Villa

Holiday Blues

Christmas night

    holiday movies
    everyone smiles
    around the tree

blinking lights

    covid lockdown
    stars in the sky
    unmasked

of the ambulance

    all seated
    for a family feast
    his shortness of breath

Christine L. Villa
Claire Vogel Camargo

Inheritance

parting clouds

> *all that's left*
> *after the rain*
> *lost fingerprints*

a last whisper

> funeral
> rehearsing dialogues
> I can never say

through a mask

> *romancing the will*
> *our fantasies*
> *of who gets what*

Christine L. Villa
Peter Jastermsky

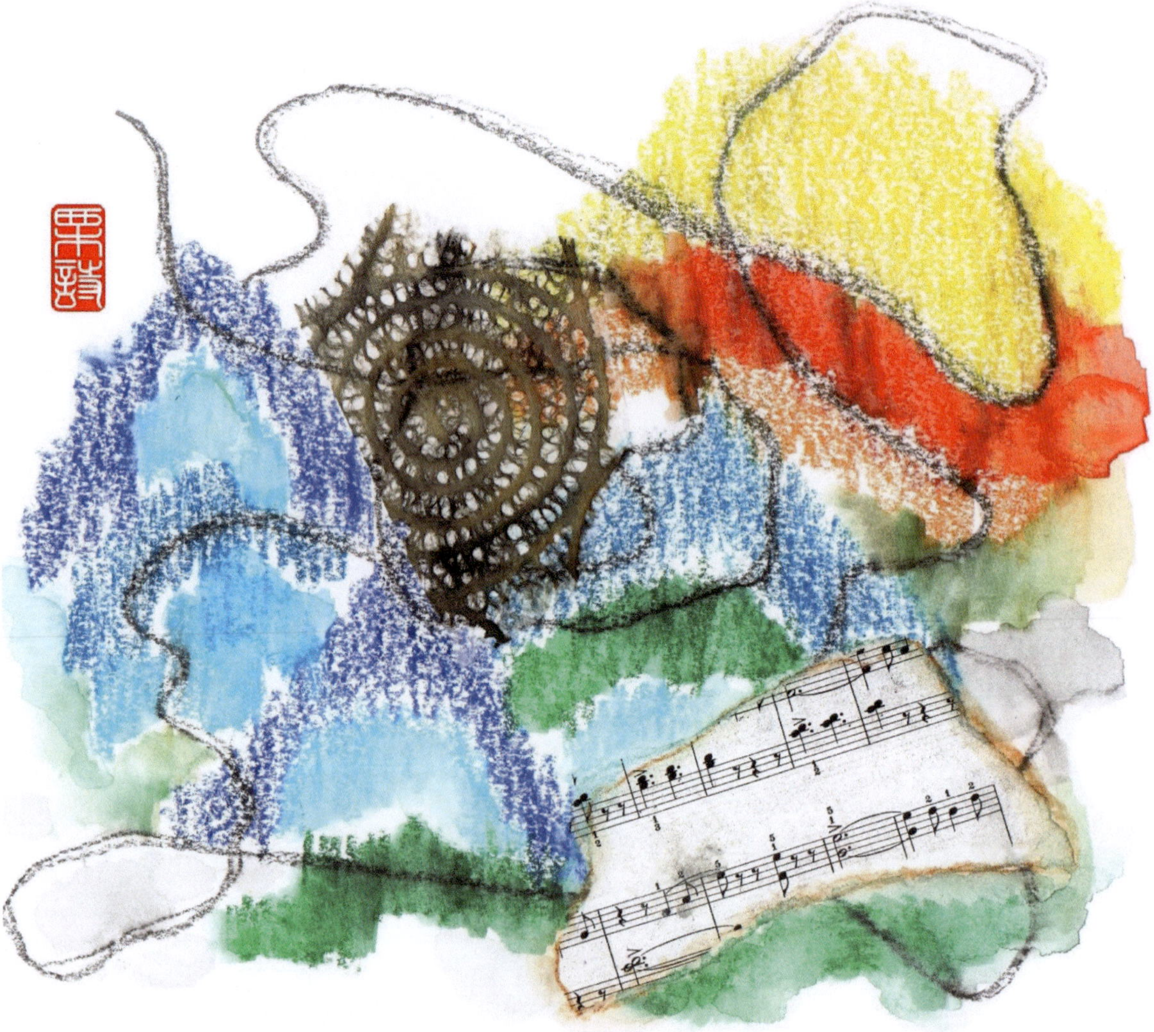

Depths of the Heart

snow-capped peaks

    misty fog
    memories of father
    revisit me

a soft light filters

    blowing curtains
    morning sun shines
    a child's crayon drawing

into the canyon's depths

    ancestral home
    an old music box
    in the attic

Jay Friedenberg
Christine L. Villa

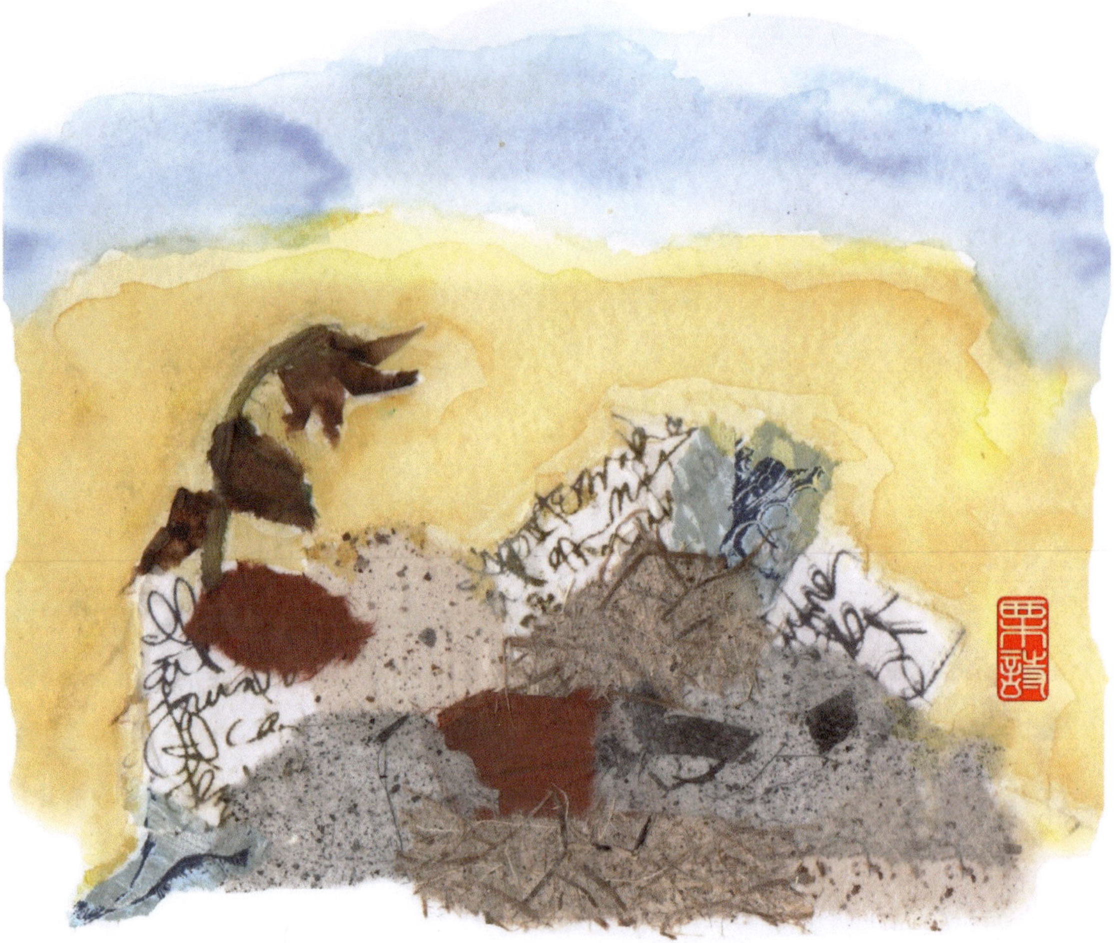

Broken Peace

Born into War

distant shelling

> *overcast skies*
> *a stream of cars*
> *leaves the city*

the gentle undulation

> *maternity hospital*
> *a baby carriage*
> *spins a wheel*

of blue and yellow

> *town square*
> *kneeling on cold stone*
> *to pray*

Jay Friedenberg
Christine L. Villa

Flight Paths

beachcombing

*frantic escape
no room for everything
in a backpack*

so many shells

*spreading dawn
an abandoned apartment
fills with light*

broken

*missing home
memories trapped
in the rubble*

John Hawkhead
Christine L. Villa

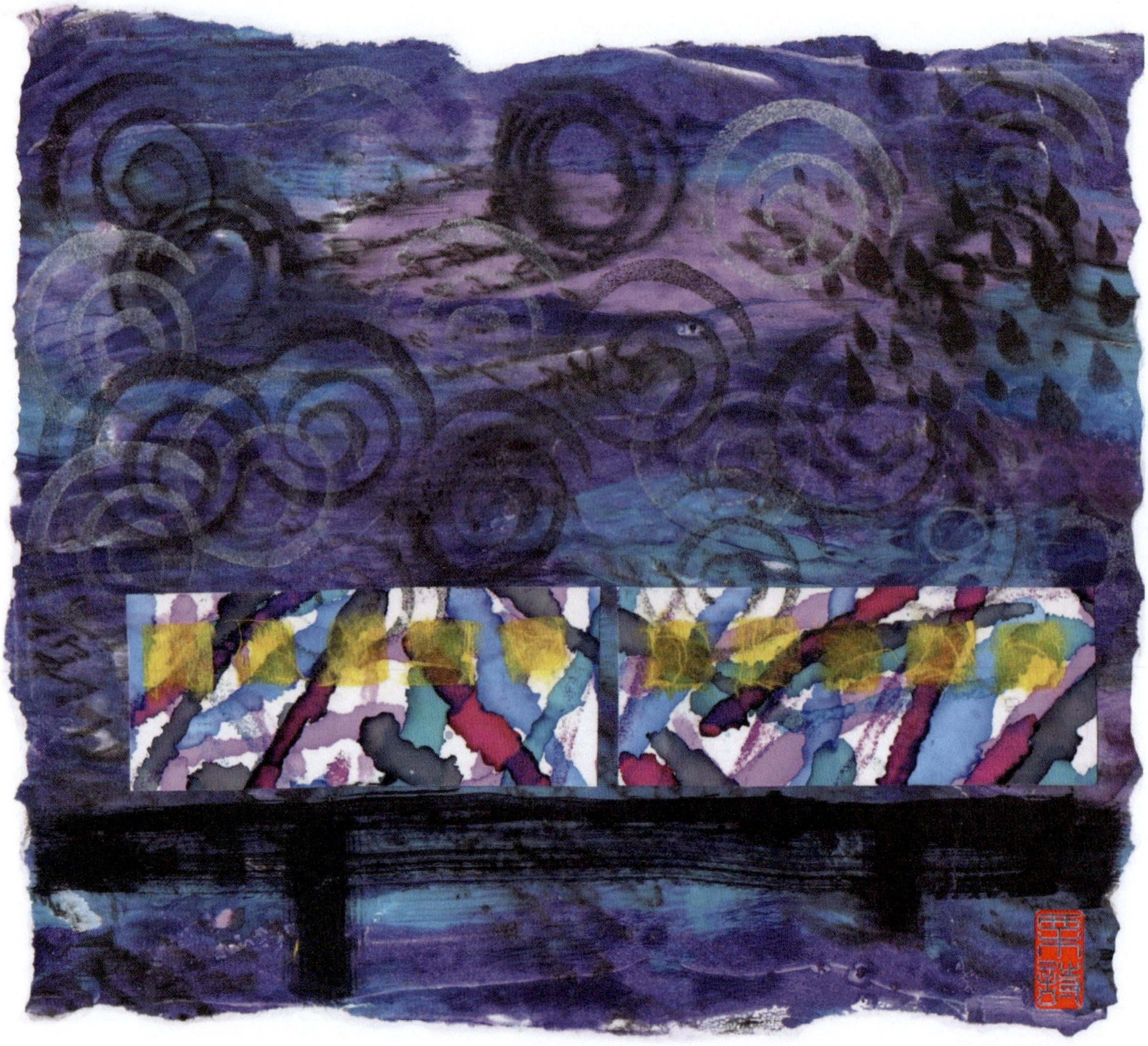

Broken Peace

forgotten lullaby . . .

*refugees piled up
on top of each other
train to Poland*

on the tin roof

*smell of gunpowder
each passing moment
a cold wave*

tapping rain

*sobbing child
at the port of entry
only strangers*

Milan Rajkumar
Christine L. Villa

In the Aftermath

another page

> *war-torn country*
> *one more child loses*
> *a father*

on the calendar . . .

> *chrysanthemums*
> *in yellow and white*
> *—a silenced hymn*

ashen sky

> *refugee tent*
> *the sound of bombs*
> *still in their heads*

Geethanjali Rajan
Christine L. Villa

A Spark of Hope

refugee exodus

*broken bridge
an old woman carries
her wounded dog*

fireflies flicker

*evacuation
mother's marmalade jar
in the debris*

in the dark forest

*air raid sirens
in the basement
a girl sings*

Arvinder Kaur
Christine L. Villa

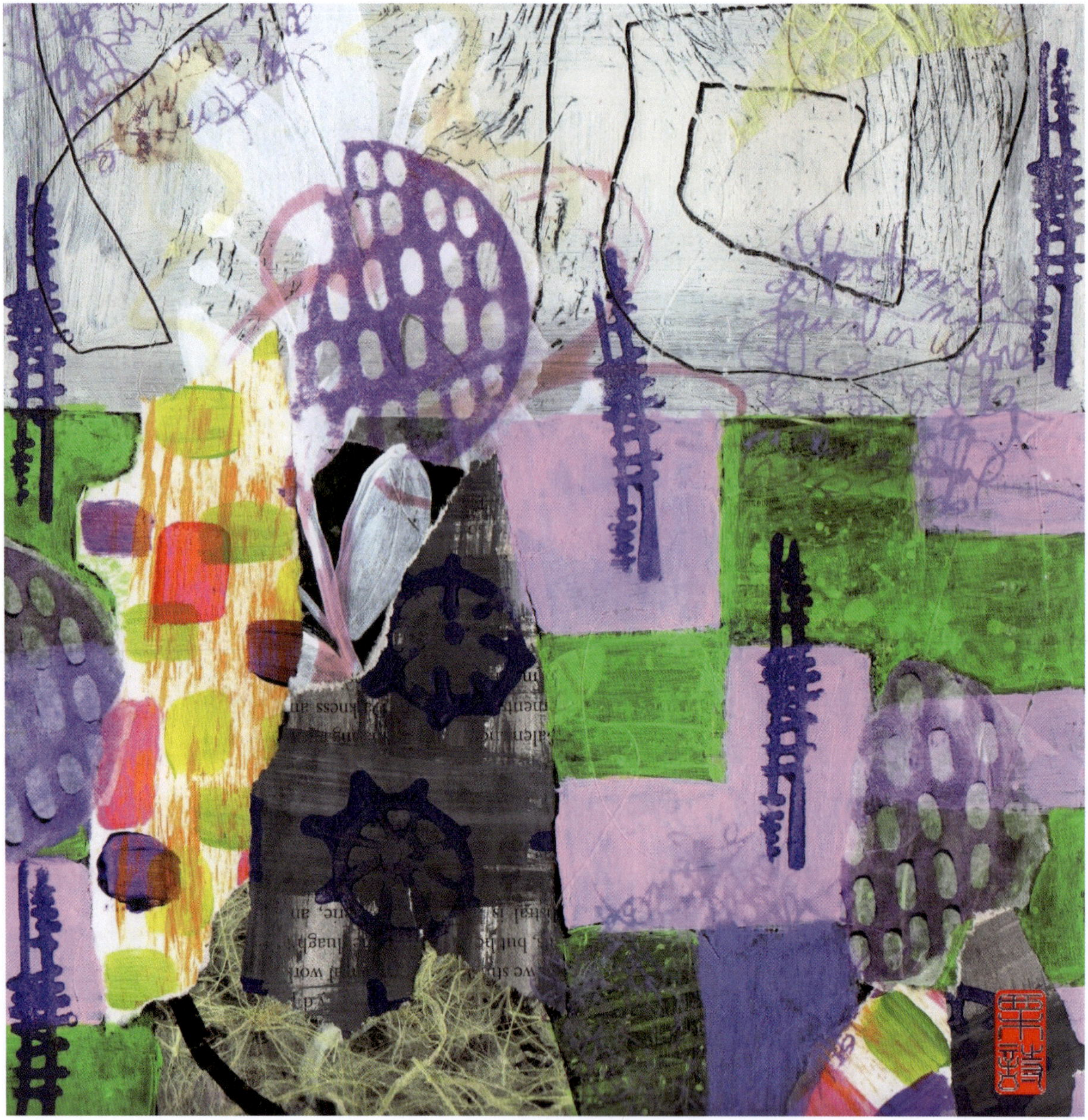

Sun Dog

good news—

warm clothes
at the border crossing
sunrise

hearing the brush

   hole in the sky
   still some space
   for a miracle

of geese wings

his first words
in a foreign language
murmuring brook

Meik Blöttenberger
Christine L. Villa

have killed the
Do you still
everything the
but these two,
such strength

After

Ancient Call

sidewalk cracks

> *the memory*
> *of an old love song*
> *skeleton leaves*

the emptiness

> *within reach*
> *of the hawk's cry*
> *scattered feathers*

going nowhere

> *hollow nest*
> *no one waits to hear*
> *my footsteps*

Tom Clausen
Christine L. Villa

Empty Bottle

long summer night

> *windows wide*
> *biting frost hard*
> *to imagine*

an old man nibbling

> a faraway gaze
> his LP record
> on repeat

a toothpick

> *unfinished meal*
> *another shot*
> *of whiskey*

Christine L. Villa
Al Peat

After

icy sunrise

   pain memory
   i disassociate from
   my limbs

the cold touch

   anniversary
   the wedding ring still
   on my finger

of his urn

   the weight
   of dew-soaked leaves
   holding me together

Christine L. Villa
Kirsten Cliff Elliot

Missing

remembering her

   another wish
   a dry clink
   in the well

without the feeling

   worn-out couch
   no more nights
   of waiting

empty seedpod

   age spots
   fill her face
   cold moon

Christine L. Villa
Billy Antonio

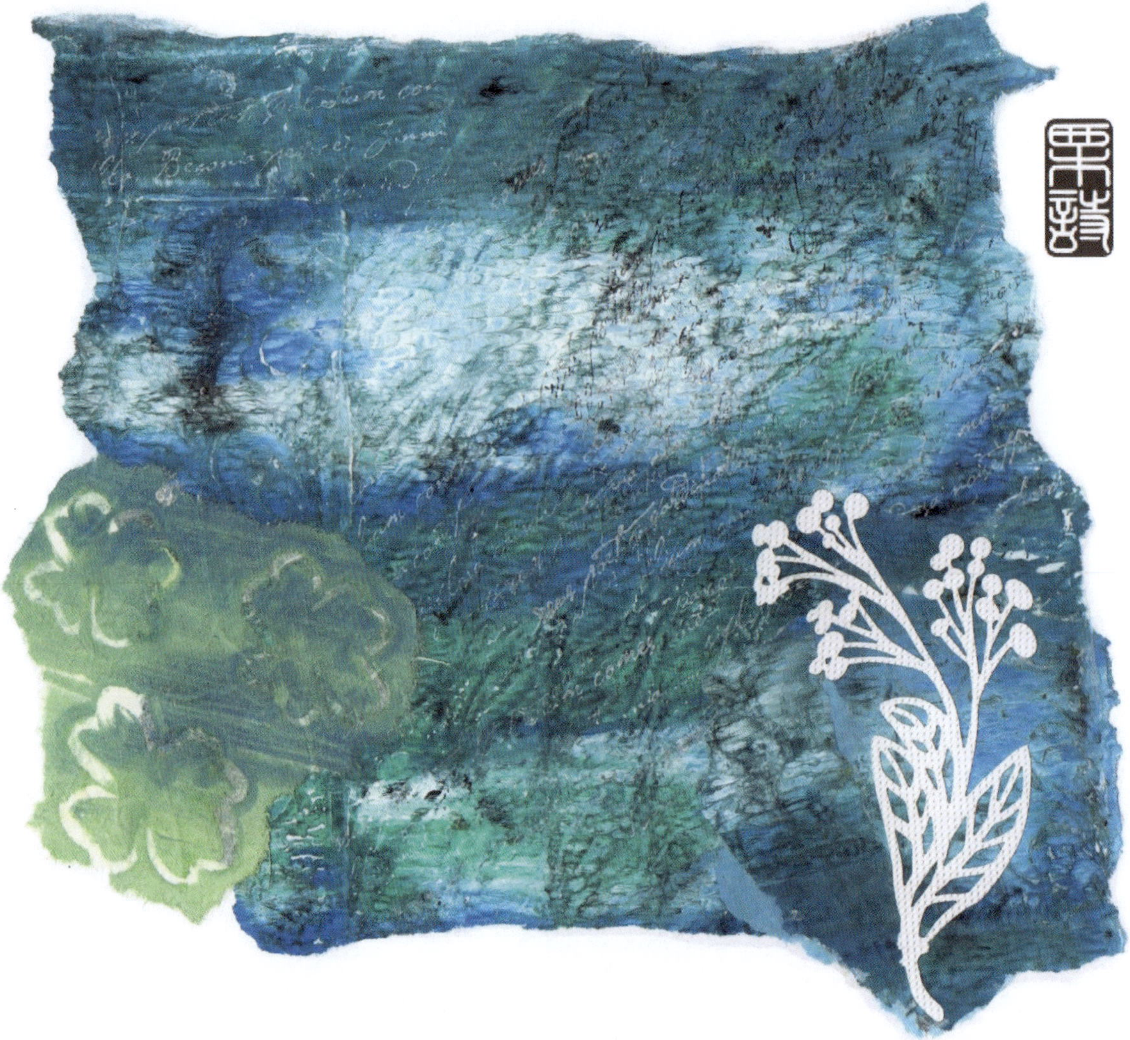

Uncharted

roadside flowers

> *first day alone*
> *the fresh smell*
> *after the rain*

their seeds sailing

> prairie horizon
> ever distant
> as we near

to a better life

> *four-leaf clover*
> *the message*
> *of a birdsong*

George Swede
Christine L. Villa

Naked Heart

wearing his shirt

*before dawn
I wrap the moment
in make believe*

straight from the drier

*memories
freshly-picked roses
from our garden*

winter sun

*a new day
I give myself another
last chance*

Christine L. Villa
Barbara Sayre

Out of the Box

no emails

   long winter dusk
   the quiet tick tick ticking
   of my dad's gold watch

she fills her window box

   her never-worn dress
   hangs outside the closet
   spring thaw

with zinnias

   left and right
   of the garden path
   summer butterflies

Christine L. Villa
Linda Papanicolaou

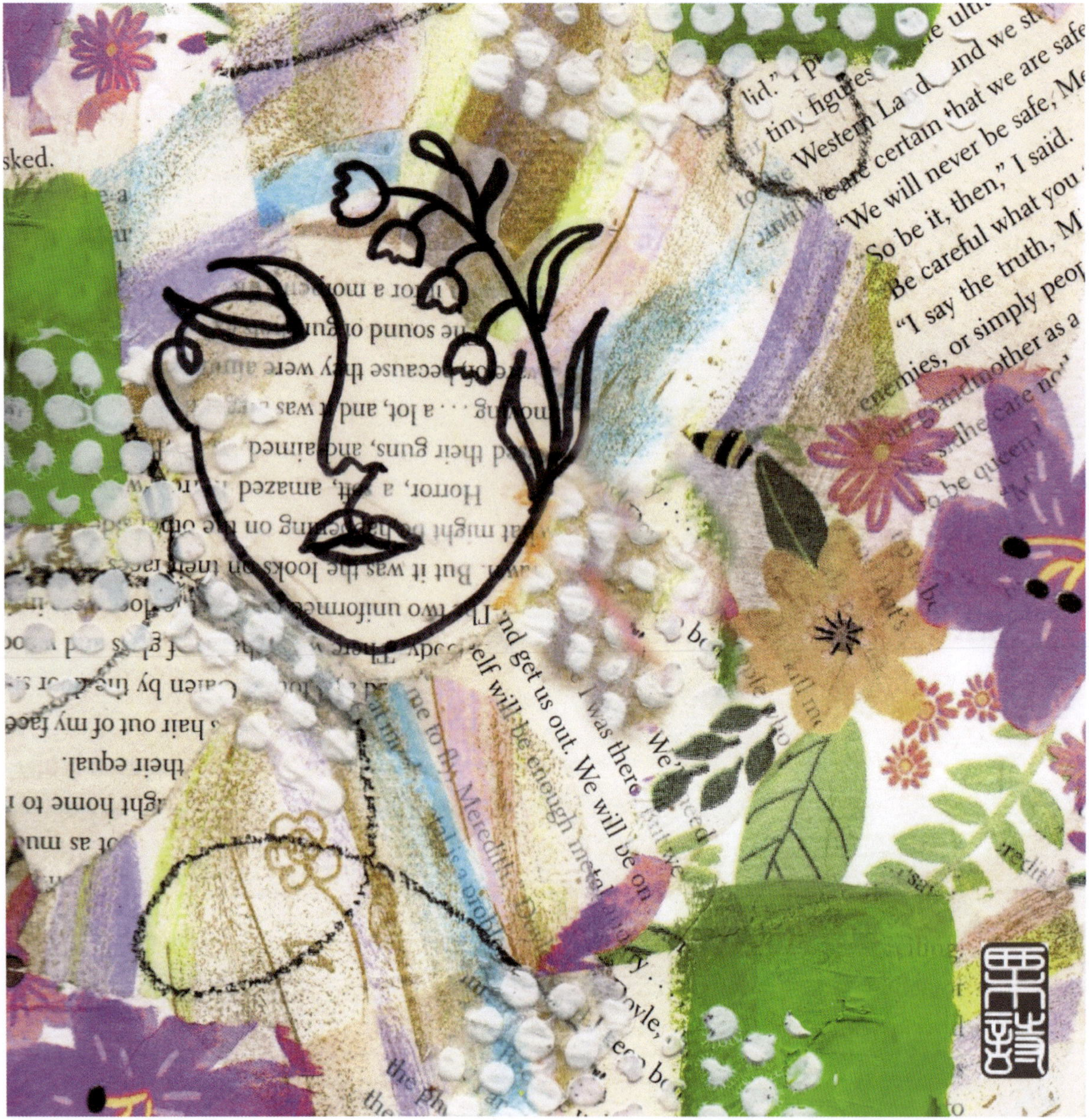

New Beginnings

Written in Sand

head in the clouds

coastal air
my thoughts roll
with the waves

like the day moon

this waiting
the poetry inside me
lights up the dark

here, yet not there

streaks of foam
cling to the reef
what's left unsaid

Carole MacRury
Christine L. Villa

On the Verge

the silence

> *just the buzz*
> *of a fluorescent light*
> *unopened letter*

before the answer

> dusk
> clouds morph
> into crickets

moonflower buds

> *first star*
> *the gentle squeeze*
> *of his hand*

Julie Schwerin
Christine L. Villa

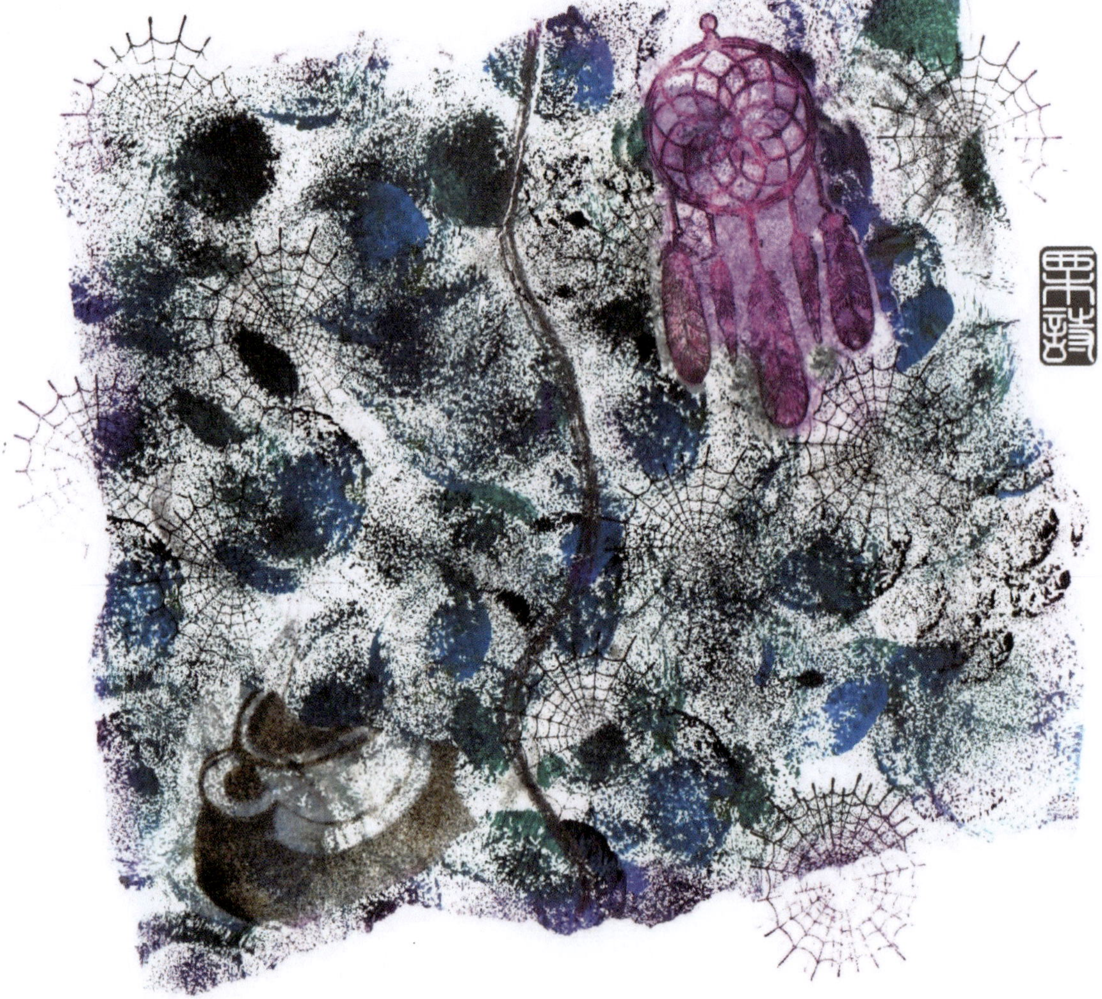

What Lies Ahead

moonlight

*tracing our scars
the length
of our nights*

sharing a teapot

distant howls
still waiting for that
phone call

and the silence

*darkness . . .
black spiders crawl
into my dreams*

Christine L. Villa
Jayashree Maniyil

Wisp

the way her nightdress

*balmy breeze
another rose petal
unfurls*

brushes her knees

*morning prayers
Hail Marys whispered
at the prie-dieu*

winter plum

*closed butterfly wings
I hold my breath
for your answer*

Terri L. French
Christine L. Villa

Vortex

peony blooms

   dog days
   the watering can
   rusted through

prayers

   night vigil
   crossing out
   the calendar

swinging in the breeze

   miracle worker
   He tells me
   I can walk on water

Christine L. Villa
Susan Furst

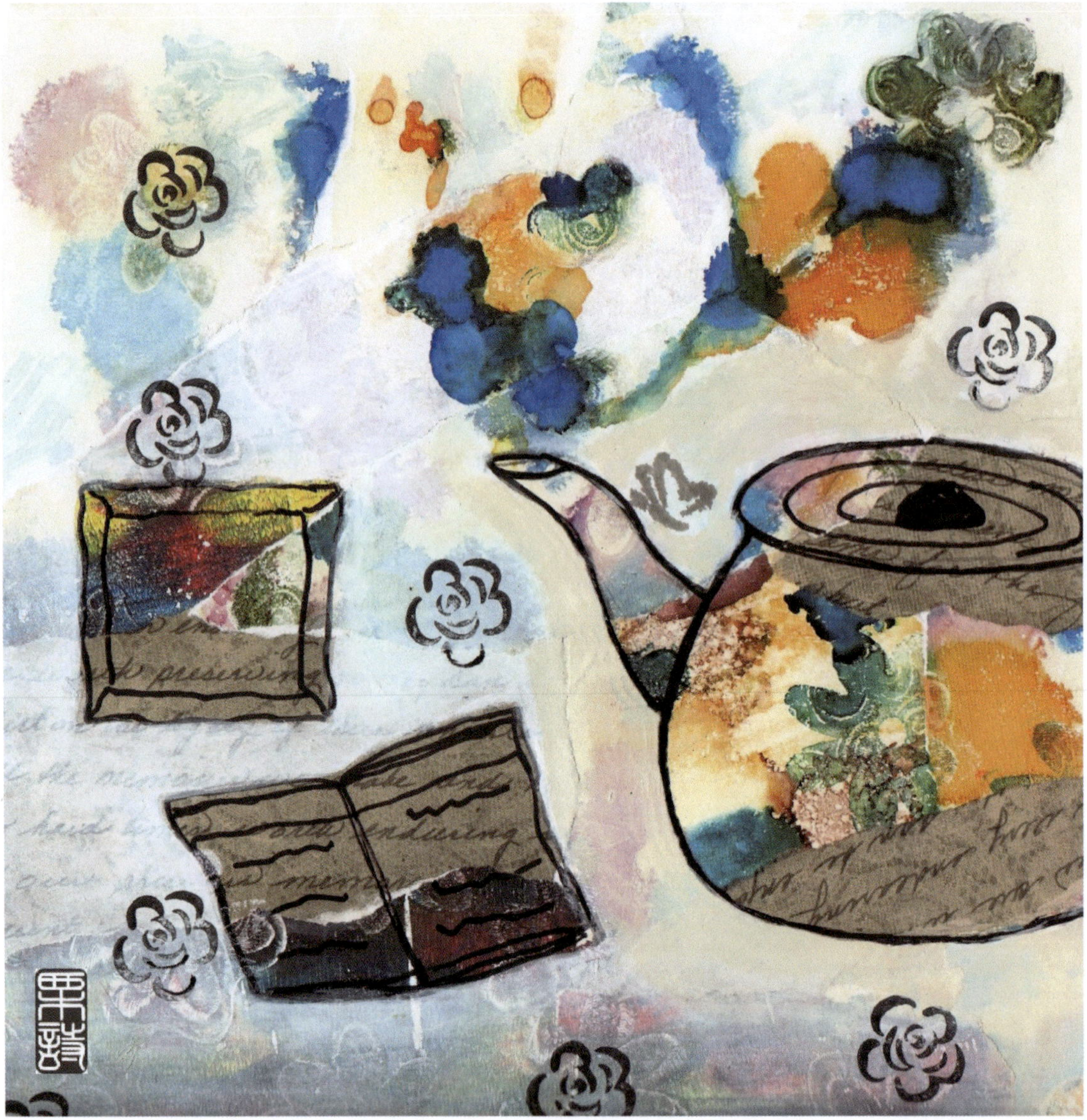

As it Heals

brass kettle

*stirring coffee
the noise I make
inside my head*

pouring my heart out

*morning diary
the rising steam
of my story*

to my reflection

*butterfly wings
I gently kiss the child
in an old photo*

Jackie Chou
Christine L. Villa

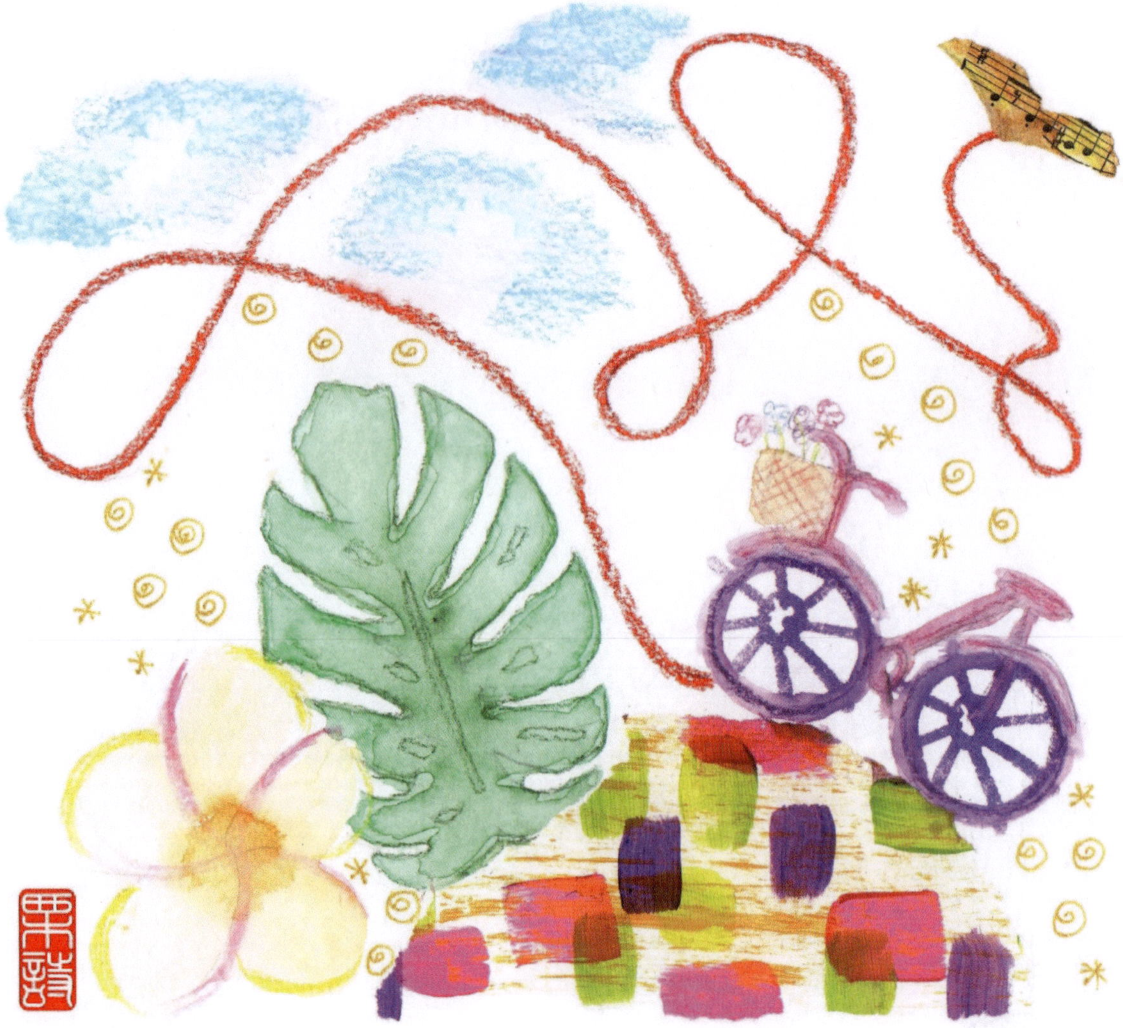

Island Visit

blossom trails

   roundabout route
   closer and closer
   to a sparrow's song

finding a way

   spring sky
   every turn becomes
   our new gravity

into my heart

   finally home
   I turn a rock and paint
   a frangipani

Joanna Ashwell
Christine L. Villa

New Beginnings

midnight oil

   rabbit hole
   unfound answers
   on the internet

at the strike of a match

   morning tea
   my future
   brighter

fireflies

   light switch
   a new entry
   in my journal

Susan Furst
Christine L. Villa

On the Other Side

fly fishing

> *mackerel sky*
> *I cast a random wish*
> *out loud*

an eagle follows

> *without wings*
> *a white feather*
> *catches the wind*

the river's bend

> *shifting clouds*
> *sunlight at the top*
> *of a mountain*

Marilyn Ashbaugh
Christine L. Villa

Afterword

In some ways, putting together an anthology sounds like a no-brainer. The usual suspects make it seem simple: *Best Science Fiction Stories* or *Fifty Contemporary American Poets*. Why, there's so much masterful work out there, an editor could probably compile Volume Two out of all the work they couldn't stuff into the original. It's a problem of quality *and* quantity. Six years ago, this book would not have been possible.

With *How the Wind Moves*, we have the first anthology of a new short form, the split sequence, that in a few brief years has grown far beyond one poet's feverish vision. It's a bold move. Dozens of writers, some admittedly allergic to linked forms, have shared their own narrative worlds within the split sequence format. Through acts of collaboration, a community is created and nurtured. It is to editor Christine L. Villa's credit that she has championed this new poetic experiment by publishing the first book of collaborative split sequences, and now, this anthology.

As the founder of the split sequence form, I invite you to join the narrative.

—Peter Jastermsky

Participating Poets

Cynthia Anderson
Yucca Valley, California, USA
Facebook: @cynthialouiseanderson
Website: www.cynthiaandersonpoet.com

Billy Antonio
Laoac, Philippines
Facebook: @billy.t.antonio.5
Instagram: @billytamondongantonio

Marilyn Ashbaugh
Edwardsburg, Michigan, USA
Facebook: @marilyn.ashbaugh
Instagram: *@ashbaugh108*

Hifsa Ashraf
Rawalpindi, Pakistan
Facebook: @hifsa.ashraf.921
Twitter: @hifsays

Joanna Ashwell
Barnard Castle, United Kingdom

Meik Blöttenberger
Hanover, Pennsylvania, USA
Instagram: @bluesawdust

Susan Burch
Hagerstown, Maryland, USA
Facebook: @susan.burch.923
Instagram: @susan.burch.923

Claire Vogel Camargo
Austin, Texas, USA
Facebook: @claire.v.camargo
Instagram: @claire.v.camargo
Twitter: @clairevcam1

Pris Campbell
Lake Worth, Florida, USA
Facebook: @pris.campbell
Website: www.poeticinspire.com

Hemapriya Chellappan
Pune, Maharashtra, India
Facebook: @hemaThetwisTedbrainS360
Instagram: @art_hemapriya
Twitter: @art_hemapriya

Christina Chin
Subang Jaya, Malaysia
Facebook: @christina.chin.3958
Instagram: @christina_zygby22
Twitter: @Christina_haiku
Website: haikuzyg.blogspot.com
   christinachin99blog.wordpress.com

Jackie Chou
Pico Rivera, California, USA
Facebook: @jackie.chou.167

Tom Clausen
Ithaca, New York, USA
Facebook: @tom.clausen.583
Instagram: @tomclausen47

Kirsten Cliff Elliot
Tyne and Wear, England
Facebook: @bookfuelled
Instagram: @bookfuelled
Twitter: @bookfuelled

Terri L. French
Huntsville, Alabama, USA
Facebook: @TerriHaleFrench
Instagram: @terri.l.french
Website: www.terrilfrenchhaiku.com

Jay Friedenberg
Tuckahoe, New York, USA
Facebook: @jay.friedenberg
Twitter: @JayFriedenberg

Susan Beth Furst
Fishersville, Virginia, USA
Facebook: @susan.furst.3
Instagram @sueshaikus @haikuukulele
Website: paperwhistlepress.com
        beautifuldefect.com

Sherry Grant
Aukland, New Zealand
Facebook: @sherry.grant.503
Instagram: @sherry.grant
Twitter: @SherryGMusic
Website: www.artsinfinitypress.com

Hazel Hall
Aranda, Australia
Facebook: @hazel.hall.7

John Hawkhead
Bradford on Avon, Wiltshire, England
Instagram: @HaikuHawk
Twitter: @HawkheadJohn

Tia Haynes
Lakewood, Ohio, USA
Facebook: @tia.haynes.5
Instagram: @adaliahaiku
Twitter: @adalia_haiku

Peter Jastermsky
Morongo Valley, California, USA
Facebook: @peterjastermsky

Carol Judkins
Carlsbad, California, USA
Facebook: @carol.judkins

Arvinder Kaur
Chandigarh, India
Facebook: @arvinder.kaur.14
Instagram: @arvinderk8
Twitter: @arvinder8

Mary Kendall
Chapel Hill, North Carolina, USA
Facebook: @mary.kendall.33
Website: www.apoetintime.com

Deborah P Kolodji
Temple City, California, USA
Facebook: @dkolodji
Twitter @dkolodji

Michael Henry Lee
Saint Augustine, Florida, USA
Facebook: @michaelhenry.lee.9

Michael H. Lester
Los Angeles, California, USA
Facebook: @mhlester
Instagram: @michael_h_lester
Twitter: @mhlester
Website: michaelhlester-poet.weebly.com

Chen-ou Liu
Ajax, Ontario, Canada
Twitter: @ericcoliu
Website: chenouliu.blogspot.com

Carole MacRury
Point Roberts, Washington, USA
Facebook: @cmacrury

Jayashree Maniyil
Facebook: @jayashree.maniyil
Instagram: @jayashree_maniyil

Linda Papanicolaou
Palo Alto, California, USA
Facebook: @paplinda

Vandana Parashar
Panchkula, India
Instagram: @_vandana0201
Twitter: @vandana020175

Al Peat
Biddulph, United Kingdom
Facebook: @profile.php?id=100074354497920

Geethanjali Rajan
Chennai, India
Facebook: @geethanjali.rajan.5
Twitter: @haikaifan

Mila Rajkumar
Imphal, India
Facebook: @rajkumar.milan

Dave Read
Calgary, Alberta, Canada
Facebook: @dave.read.75873
Twitter: @davereapoetry

Bryan Rickert
Belleville, Illinois, USA
Facebook: @bryan.rickert.3

Bona M. Santos
Los Angeles, California, USA

Barbara Sayre
Winchester, Tennessee, USA
Facebook: @barbara.tate.315

Julie Schwerin
Sun Prairie, Wisconsin, USA
Facebook: @julie.warther.5

Robin Anna Smith
Middletown, Delaware, USA
Instagram: @komadorihaiku
Link tree: @komadorihaiku

Debbie Strange
Winnipeg, Manitoba, Canada
Instagram: @debbiemstrange
Twitter: @Debbie_Strange

Alan Summers
Chippenham, Wiltshire, England
Facebook: @alan.summers.92372
Instagram: @haikutec
Twitter: @haikutec
Website: www.callofthepage.org

George Swede
Toronto, Ontario, Canada
Facebook: @george.swede.7
Instagram: @george.swede
Twitter: @GeorgeSwede

Elisa Theriana
Bandung, Indonesia
Facebook: @Elisatheriana
Instagram: @Elisatheriana
Twitter: @Elisatheriana

Publishing Credits

Some of the collaborative split sequences were first published by the following:

The Bamboo Hut
Behold
Cantos
Failed Haiku
Fireflies' Light
Frameless Sky
Frogpond
hedgerow: a journal of small poems
MacQueen's Quinterly
Mulberry Literary
Narrow Road
Northern California Publishers and Authors in the anthology
    All Holidays: Volume two
Poetry Pea Journal
Prune Juice
The Quills
Scarlet Dragonfly Journal
Verse-Virtual

The haiku "cloud formation" was first published in *The Bluebird's Cry* by Christine L. Villa.

Collaborative split sequences that were first published in *How the Wind Moves* are the following:

"Imprints"
"All It Takes"
"Spring Rendezvous"
"The Morning After"
"Stuck"
"Cracks"
"Signpost"
"Circling the Drain"
"After Lucinda?"
"Self-Soothing"
"Depths of the Heart"
"Flight Paths"
"In the Aftermath"
"A Spark of Hope"
"Sun Dog"
"Out of the Box"
"Wisp"
"Island Visit"

About the Editor/Poet

Christine L. Villa is a Filipino-American who lives in North Highlands, California with her Maltipoo named Haiku. As an all-around creative explorer, she is a children's book author, haiku and tanka poet, publisher, speaker, photographer, mixed media artist, and crafter. Several of her poems, photos, and artwork have won awards and recognition. She is the founder of Purple Cotton Candy Arts, a fast-growing business that offers publishing services to children's book authors. She is also the founding editor and publisher of *Frameless Sky* (a short-form poetry video journal) and Velvet Dusk Publishing for haiku and tanka chapbooks and full-length books. You can learn more about her work by visiting the websites below.

Website: www.christinevilla.com
Picture Book Publication: www.purplecottoncandyarts.com
Poetry Website: blossomrain.blogspot.com
Poetry Journal: framelesssky.weebly.com
Poetry Publication: velvetduskpublishing.weebly.com

Printed in Great Britain
by Amazon